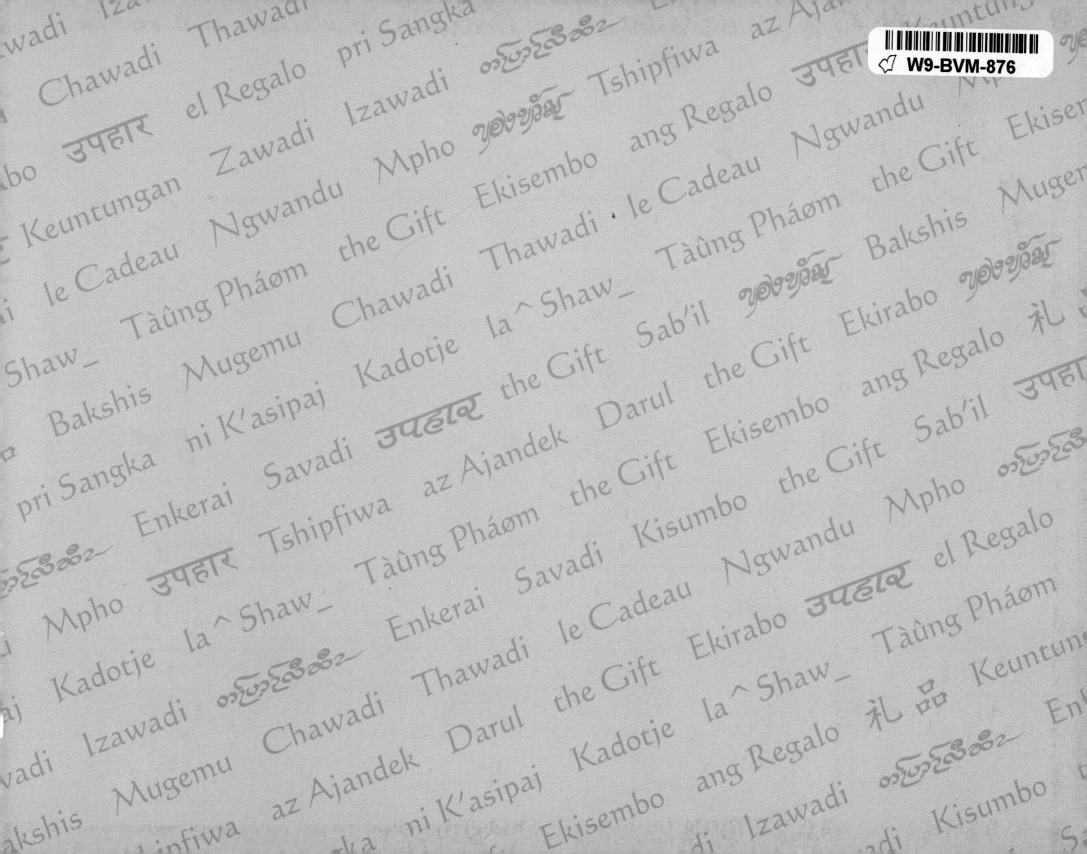

W9-BVM-876

the Gift

HEIFER PROJECT INTERNATIONAL

the Gift

A WORLD SOLUTION TO HUNGER AND POVERTY

BY MATT AND SUSAN BRADLEY

Text Editors - Anna H. Bedford, Jack Schnedler, Marcia Schnedler, Ann Waldo, Judy Wilbourn
Picture Editors - Matt and Susan Bradley
Design and Prepress Production - Matt Bradley
Production/Design Consultant - John Houser
Print Production Coordinator - John Coghlan

Published by Bradley Publishing, Little Rock, Arkansas, in cooperation with Heifer Project International, Inc.
© 1998 by Heifer Project International, Inc.   Photographs © 1998 by Matt Bradley

All rights reserved. Published 1998
Printed and bound in South Korea
02 01 00 99   4 3 2 1
Reproduction of the whole or any part of the contents without written permission is prohibited.

Inquiries should be addressed to:

Heifer Project International, Inc.
1015 Louisiana Street
P.O. Box 808
Little Rock, AR 72203-0808

Phone (501) 376-6836 or (800) 422-0474
Fax (501) 376-8906
Web Site: http://www.heifer.org

Library of Congress Catalogue Card Number: 98-92641
ISBN 0-940716-04-6; 0-940716-05-4 (pbk)

End Sheets: *The Gift* translated in languages from 38 Heifer Project countries
Page 1: daughters of an HPI farmer holding week-old goats, Salgaon village near Goa, India
Page 2-3: alpaca herd grazing near the village of Inca Katurapi, Bolivia
Page 5: Akha girls with a calf, San Makhet, northern Thailand
Page 8: the camel Rupa (The Beautiful One) surrounded by children from Dhani Ghadawali, India

CONTENTS

HEIFER PROJECT INTERNATIONAL
PROJECT COUNTRIES

Heifer Project Animals

Alpacas	Horses
Bees	Llamas
Camels	Mules
Chickens	Ostriches
Cows	Oxen
Donkeys	Pigeons
Ducks	Pigs
Earthworms	Rabbits
Elephants	Sheep
Fish	Silk Worms
Geese	Snails
Goats	Water Buffalo
Guinea Pigs	Yaks

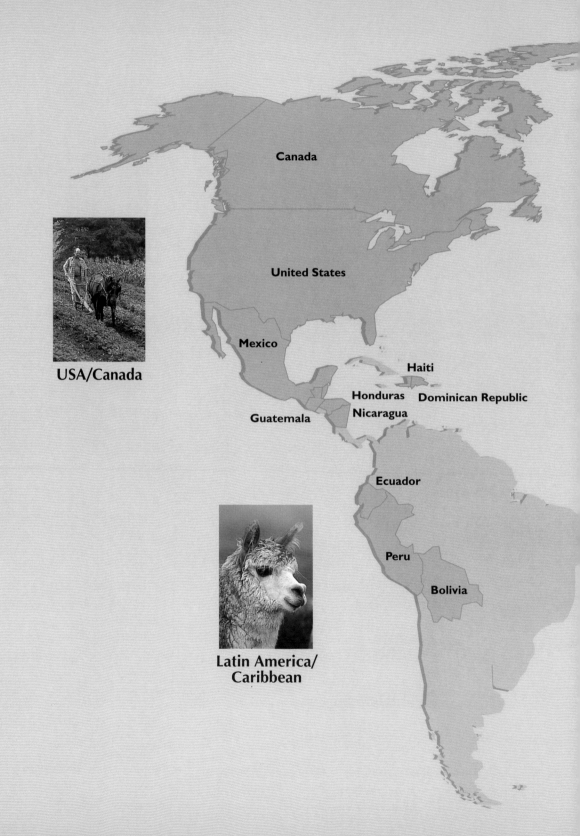

USA/Canada

Latin America/
Caribbean

Central/
Eastern Europe

Poland
Ukraine
Slovakia
Bosnia
Romania
Albania

Russia

Afghanistan
Pakistan

Nepal

China

D.P.R. Korea
South Korea

Asia/
South Pacific

Ghana
Cameroon

Uganda

India

Bangladesh
Thailand

Laos

Vietnam

Cambodia

Philippines

Sri Lanka

Kenya
Tanzania

Papua New Guinea

Zambia

Indonesia

Zimbabwe

Africa/
Near East

Mozambique

South Africa

7

As I've visited families around the world and in rural and urban areas of the United States, I have felt a special bond of friendship with them. I've found that parents everywhere share many of the same dreams.

Parents want their children to be happy and healthy. They dream about giving their children an education so they will have a full, meaningful life. Parents work hard to achieve these goals.

Dreams are destroyed when, despite parents' best efforts, hunger and poverty take their toll. Far too many of the world's children have little to look forward to in their future.

That's why I have a special place in my heart for Heifer Project International—an organization that works tirelessly to build a better future for the world's forgotten families. For more than 50 years, Heifer Project has been helping families—more than four million of them—to realize their dreams. With gifts of HPI livestock and training, families can feed their children, send them to school and start them on the road to becoming global citizens.

Heifer Project is courageously addressing some of the most difficult problems facing our world today—ending hunger, preserving the environment, empowering women, and building strong, self-reliant families and communities.

This book brings you face to face with some of these families. In their eyes you will see hope. Their stories will renew your commitment to making the world a happier, safer place for everyone.

I join you in celebrating the valuable work of Heifer Project International. Together, we will continue to work for a just and peaceful world.

Hillary Rodham Clinton

Hillary Rodham Clinton, First Lady
United States of America

ACKNOWLEDGMENTS

BOOK SPONSORS

The Walton Family Foundation

NationsBank

Heifer International Foundation

Ursula Bartel
Jerry and Anna Bedford
Margaret, Susan and Richard Eyre
Marvel Lund

HEIFER PROJECT INTERNATIONAL COVENANT AGENCIES

African Methodist Episcopal Church

American Baptist Church

American Friends Service Committee

Church of the Brethren World Ministries Commission

Christian Church (Disciples of Christ)

Presiding Bishop's Fund of the Episcopal Church

Evangelical Lutheran Church in America

Mennonite Central Committee

National Catholic Rural Life Conference

Presbyterian Church (USA) Hunger Program

United Church Board for World Ministries

United Methodist Committee on Relief

WHAT IS THE GIFT?   For thousands of hungry families each year, it is a new beginning through the gift of livestock and training. With the support of congregations and many valued part-ner organizations, this gift of self-reliance and dignity is the precious opportunity that Heifer Project International has spread to families in 115 countries since 1944.

The Gift tells disarmingly simple stories of a few of them. Matt and Susan Bradley visited fami-lies in North and South America, Europe, Africa and Asia. The images captured by Matt's camera and the hope-filled stories recorded in Susan's notebook are as varied as the faces in the pictures—and as similar as the common human desire for a better life.

In every village and hamlet, Matt and Susan found that in the most difficult circumstances, men and women find ingenious ways to make the most of what little they have. By some standards, the amount of money a small jug of milk (*right*) might bring to a woman in India may be insignificant. But to her family, it can mean the difference between extreme poverty and meeting their basic needs.

The families who have received assistance also enjoy the privilege of giving one or more of their animal's offspring to another family in need. Thus, every recipient becomes a donor. This "passing on the gift"—the heart of Heifer Project's faith-based mission—spreads the security of better nutri-tion and income from milk, eggs, fiber, labor or other benefits.

With a reliable source of food and income, hope for the future grows. So does respect for the value and dignity of others. Families begin working to educate their children, build up their commu-nity, preserve natural resources and improve the environment for generations to come.

Ultimately, the gift is the promise of a brighter future—mutual respect and a better quality of life for people everywhere.

Jo Luck

President and CEO
Heifer Project International

ASIA/
SOUTH PACIFIC

Asia and the South Pacific include more than two-thirds of the world's villages. Together, China and India comprise more than one-third of the world's population. Many of the vibrant people in this part of the world, including Buddhists, Muslims, Confucians and Hindus, are building modern societies on ancient foundations.

Large sectors of many countries in the region are experiencing rapid economic growth. However, much of the population continues to trudge through age-old challenges of sustaining adequate food production. Many efforts over the years that have focused solely on increasing productivity of food crops have left out the most important part of the equation....people. These people have needs, hopes and dreams. Heifer Project programs provide locally appropriate education to farmers and their family members. We tailor much of the training to meet the various linguistic and schedule needs of women and girls. This is one of the key factors that reduces population growth, as well as equitably and effectively meeting the needs of families and communities today.

Thriving agriculture is a catalyst for broad-based economic growth and improved quality of life. In China, members of the Hongya Dairy Project use profits from their milk production to improve family nutrition, education and housing quality, as well as upgrade agricultural equipment like water pumps for irrigation *(left)*. In the Philippines and Indonesia, two countries with large HPI programs not featured in this book, the results are just as significant.

The images that follow unfold a story of interdependence among Heifer Project donors, volunteers, program countries and the communities we serve. No country or project stands alone. All are part of a larger plan embodied in the Bible: "As each one has received a *special* gift, employ it in serving one another, as good stewards of the manifold grace of God" *(1 Peter 4:10)*.

Dr. Robert K. Pelant
Program Director, Asia/South Pacific

CHINA

In a country with 20 percent of the world's mouths to feed but only 7 percent of the planet's arable land, can a few geese make a meaningful difference? Just ask Zhong Xueying *(far right)*.

"I don't have other skills and can't do heavy physical work," says the Sichuan Province farm woman. "Raising and selling geese brings in money for food and clothing. In just one year, my income has more than doubled."

Zhong's success story is merely one among thousands told by thriving Heifer Project participants in China, a tribute to the nation's industrious people and HPI's philosophy that the secret to lasting change is building relationships at the grassroots level. Livestock such as ducks, geese and rabbits presents a low-cost, high-yield opportunity for China's farmers who possess limited resources but unlimited energy and ambition. As land has shifted from collective farms to individual ownership, having these small animals helps farmers work toward self-reliance.

The ducklings mobbing eight-year-old Li Jun Cai *(near right)*, nephew of an HPI farmer in Sichuan Province, will reach their market weight of four pounds in two months.

"In the future I want to expand even more—set up a bigger business with production, marketing and processing— the whole dragon."

Ren Xuping
HPI Farmer

STAGGERING NUMBERS   Almost one billion Chinese make their living from small-scale farming. Selecting livestock to address a need of such staggering proportions calls for an animal well acquainted with the principle of rapid multiplication. Farmer Li De Xian and Professor Pu Jiabi, director of HPI/China (*right*), know that rabbits fill the bill.

In 1985, HPI introduced 105 Californian and New Zealand White rabbits to four families through the DaYi County Rabbit Project in Sichuan Province. In exchange for the animals, each family agreed to pass on five offspring rabbits to neighbors. Over the next 13 years, those initial 105 rabbits exploded into more than 16,000, helping 2,750 families feed themselves and become self-reliant.

Ren Xuping, one of the original recipients, now owns properties worth $175,000, including a training school for rabbit farmers. As a result of HPI/China's training in marketing, DaYi County has become a source of quality rabbit meat and breeding stock for 15 provinces.

PASSING ON THE GIFT Recipients of Heifer Project animals are required to "pass on the gift"—that is, to share one or more of the animal's offspring. This is a serious obligation, implemented by a contract with each recipient. Heifer Project thus refers to the animals it provides as living loans.

Before anyone can receive a pass-on, he or she must qualify by learning how to care for the animal and making proper provisions for shelter, food and water.

Xu Fu Ying *(left, in blue jacket reading scale)* checks the weight of the 16th generation pass-on rabbits she is giving to Yang You Chun *(left and above, in dark red sweater)*. The animals are carefully observed and weighed to ensure the pass-on rabbits are of equal or greater quality and weight than those initially received.

Unable to read or write, Yang You Chun prepares to place her thumbprint on the contract *(above)* that commits her to pass on the gift to another person in need.

GOLDEN GOATS Zhang Chao Fu (*right and above*) was honored with the Heifer Project International Foundation Golden Talent Award in 1997 for his outstanding work with artificial insemination and crossbreeding of dairy goats in Sichuan Province. HPI crossbred goats generally produce 90 percent more milk than local breeds, while retaining their natural disease resistance and adaptation to the local environment.

The British Saanen breeding buck giving Zhang's lab coat an affectionate nibble (*right*) breeds more than 1,000 does each year. Most of his offspring stay in the township; however, some of the best male goats were shipped to the Democratic People's Republic of Korea (North Korea) in 1997.

Years ago, Zhang Chao Fu was the first to apply for HPI training classes even before any goats arrived. Now widely respected, he dedicates time to help community farmers manage their animals' health needs.

The $1,000 Golden Talent awards are divided between the recipients and their community. Zhang chose to share his by buying goats for other farmers and improving the project's artificial insemination center.

SPECTACULAR RISE   Enjoying the fruits of their labor, Li Jun Fen and her brother Li Jun Hua fire up their bamboo-fueled double wok in a Sichuan Province kitchen *(left)* considered luxurious by neighbors. The family's growth to prosperity has been nothing short of spectacular, a tribute to the resourcefulness of their hardworking father Li Zhen Pu *(above)* and a seed planted by Heifer Project.

In the early 1980s, the Li family lived in a dilapidated hut and earned only $50 a year from selling chicken eggs. In 1985, they received HPI dairy goats. By 1992, their income had rocketed to $1,200 a year by milking and marketing the goat herd.

Li later upgraded from dairy goats to Holstein cows. Each cow in his herd of five produces an average of 1,300 gallons of milk a year and gives birth to a calf. By 1994, with his annual income above $3,600, Li could afford to build a modern, two-story house.

His neighbors like to share in his success. They visit frequently to watch the color television.

RESTOCKED YAK   Yak, reminiscent of the American bison (*left*), not only survive but thrive in the high-altitude extremes of the vast Tibetan Plateau. Thick, shaggy hair protects them against winter temperatures that can plummet to -40° F, and they forage under snow more efficiently than most other livestock.

Although they work with other animals like sheep and goats, the nomadic Tibetan herders (*above*) are dependent on the yak, as they have been for 5,000 years. Unlike sheep and goats, yak can carry heavy loads—even riders—and they produce milk rich with butterfat year-round.

A 1996 winter storm killed more than half a million animals in Tibet and virtually eliminated a year of reproduction. Heifer Project, with support from the Christian Church (Disciples of Christ), responded with a major yak restocking project.

Working with the government animal breeding center, Heifer Project helps people avoid future disasters by improving their winter camp. This includes storing grasses for winter feed and ensuring good health for animals going into the harsh winter season, when a mature yak can lose up to 40 percent of its body weight.

MOBILE HOMES   With smoke from a dung fire stinging their eyes, women separate yak milk to make butter inside their tent home known as a yurt (*near right*). These black tents woven from yak hair provide shelter during the winter season, when families must relocate every month or two due to diminishing pasture quality. With all their possessions on the backs of yaks, the herders take one or two days to move.

Milking (*far right, top*) and processing the milk into food falls to the women, as does spinning yak hair into thread (*far right, bottom*). Heifer Project crossbred yaks produce three times the milk of local stock.

Like the North American Indian tribes, who are their direct descendants, Tibetans waste nothing. They use every part of the yak: meat, blood and internal organs are considered good food; coarse belly hair provides the fiber for yurts, while softer wool is woven into clothing and rope. The hide is tanned for making boots and dung is dried for fuel.

Tribal people are exempt from the Chinese government's "one couple, one child" population control policy that results in a common preference for male children. Despite the exemption, boys like six-month-old Zha Xi (*above*) are still preferred because parents believe they will be stronger workers.

INDIA

Gridlocked in poverty, India's masses still struggle for daily survival, a drama played out in slums such as Palam village in New Delhi (*far right*). While figures for India's economic growth show progress, hundreds of millions of extremely poor people are the reason why the country faces such an uphill battle. The total population of 950 million is growing at a rate of 18 million each year; half subsist on less than one dollar a day, and 48 percent are illiterate.

India's ballooning population puts incredible pressure on resources like land, food and jobs—and drives up costs. These factors stack the odds against the many Indians struggling to break out of the poverty cycle.

Increasingly, desperate villagers are leaving their meager land parcels and funneling into the cities to slums like Palam. Here, Heifer Project works to help them make a stand, but that too has been a struggle. HPI's Palam project started with 50 goats in 1992 when there was still grazing land nearby. But the pastures became new slums and thieves have whittled away at the goat herd.

Sunder Singh (*near right*) and her family own two of the remaining 10 project goats. Waste vegetables from a nearby market now provide the major food source for the animals. For millions of impoverished Indians subsisting on a diet seriously lacking in other sources of protein, only goats and their nutrient-rich milk stand between them and an even more desperate plight.

"Goats are like a living bank to these people. They can be quickly converted to cash for dowry, sickness or ceremony."

Dr. Brij Chandra
Former Director, HPI/India

ROOFTOP DAIRY   After sunset, as darkness closes in on the New Delhi slum of Palam and the din of street life slowly subsides, an aura of tranquility settles over the community. That is when the Singh family leads its goats up narrow stairs to the roof of their tiny apartment.

Bringing the animals to the roof at night allows for rare minutes of family privacy. There, the goats are milked *(left)* and also protected from local thieves.

Called by Mahatma Gandhi the "poor man's cow," a healthy goat can produce three offspring and one ton of milk each year, while subsisting mainly on vegetable waste.

HAPPY TO BE HERE   Sitting on the floor, sharing lunch trays and eating only the most basic of foods *(right)* is not demeaning when you know no other way.

Caring for the 183 children living at the Bal Rashmi Orphanage located near Jaipur with only limited resources is sometimes overwhelming. No one knows the strain better than Alice Garg *(left)*. She founded the Bal Rashmi (Children's Day) Society in 1972 to take care of four homeless children. Garg has since expanded Bal Rashmi into a major orphanage and an umbrella organization addressing many family and community development needs.

Heifer Project prefers to work in partnership with grassroots, community-based organizations like the Bal Rashmi Society. The result is much more powerful and long lasting than that of either organization working alone.

In 1984, Heifer Project sent 10 cows to Bal Rashmi, crossbred between Jersey and the local Kankrej breed specifically to withstand India's climate and disease conditions *(below, left)*. Since then, these animals and their offspring have provided milk to the children, who in return take care of the milking and feeding chores.

"Poor families do not need charity, they need support. HPI gives them the fishing rod, not the fish. That is more important."

Alice Garg *(above)*
Bal Rashmi Society

CAMEL-POWERED BOOKMOBILE With 75 percent of India's population living in rural villages, the country's literacy problem is almost unsolvable. One solution: camel power!

The children of Khebi village will be the first to tell you the camel Chetan (He Who Brings Knowledge) lives up to his name *(above)*. Chetan makes frequent stops in Khebi, pulling a library cart loaded with 2,600 books *(right)*.

Thanks to Heifer Project working through the Bal Rashmi Society, two camel libraries bring books to 24 rural villages and schools in the state of Rajasthan. More than 300 villagers regularly borrow books for a membership fee of 12 cents a month.

Librarian Mot Singh *(far right)*, raised in the Bal Rashmi Orphanage *(previous pages)*, lives on its campus with his family. He is one of seven now-grown children who benefited from Bal Rashmi and now serve on its staff, devoting their energy to helping others.

TRUE VALUE   The worth of an animal is typically measured in money, but its true value can extend far beyond the owner's pockets. In India, camels are not only breadwinners, but also instruments to change people's lives.

Gopal Lal Meena (*near right*) became disabled during a trip to Jaipur from his small farm in north-central India. A surging crowd forced him under a train, cutting off both legs. With a wife and two children to support, Meena was sinking into despair until friends told him about Heifer Project's camel cart program.

Now, thanks to the income he earns by driving his camel cart, Gopal is able to provide for his family. His outlook on life has reversed. With money earned through his camel and cart, he purchased two dairy buffalo. He now sells milk not consumed by his family at the market for additional income.

Only a few miles away in Dhani Ghadawali, it is dark but already hot at 3 A.M. when the men drive their camel carts to work at a brick factory. They work swiftly (*far right*) because they are paid by the load—71 cents per thousand bricks moved. Quitting time is 9 A.M. when the heat becomes unbearable. With a daily income of six dollars, these workers consider themselves fortunate men. Their turning point came when they received HPI camels and carts through the Bal Rashmi Society.

Before that, the men were migrant workers moving from job to job earning one dollar a day or less. Many subsisted on bootlegging and petty thievery. Because they were always on the go, schooling for their children was out of the question. Now, the 15 families of Dhani Ghadawali have increased their income six-fold, constructed permanent homes, and enrolled their children in schools—a testimonial to camel power and HPI's holistic, long-term approach.

UNLIKELY HEROINE　All three generations of the Dhuri family are thriving—you can see it in their faces (*near right*).

One catalyst for their success in southern India has been Gauri, their Heifer Project dairy buffalo (*above*) named after an Indian goddess. Living proof that beauty is in the eye of the beholder, she more than makes up for her homely appearance by providing milk to the family.

Buffalo produce an average of six quarts of milk a day per animal, and their milk is preferred to cow's because of its higher fat and protein content. Dairy production is vital to the Dhuris for steady income during both the dry and the monsoon seasons, each lasting approximately four months in this region.

Gorakha Dhuri and his brother, Bhudhaji, have used income from milk sales to build a neighborhood temple for worship and a mill for grinding grain. They've purchased an electric pump to provide year-round irrigation for their crops and a sewing machine for their sister's wedding present.

"The buffalo inspires me to work harder," says Gorakha.

FIRE FROM DUNG   During the rains when dry wood is in short supply, dung "cakes" keep the Dhuris' kitchen fire burning brightly *(near left)*.

In India, as in most developing countries, animal manure is highly valued. Besides serving as fertilizer for the fields, dried dung becomes a key fuel source in areas where wood is not available.

In the Dhuri family, it is the women's responsibility to make dung cakes *(below)*. They mix the buffalo manure with water and straw, form it into patties and leave it to dry in the sun. Resembling huge pancakes, these patties are stacked and covered to await the monsoon season.

Here, as in all of India, Heifer Project is promoting the use of biogas—a natural process in which animal manure is stored in an airtight, underground container where it produces methane. The gas is piped to the home and used for cooking and lighting. When the methane is extracted, the remaining slurry is removed and spread on gardens and fields.

NEPAL

Nestled among the accordion folds of terraced fields 60 miles north-west of Kathmandu, the village of Gurung Gaon lies near the end of the road, a situation not uncommon in a country whose northern border is defined by the Himalayan Mountains.

Because of its remoteness and an isolationist policy that lasted until the 1950s, Nepal continues to be among the world's least developed nations. Most of its people are farmers, living in isolated villages similar to Gurung Gaon. An estimated 40 percent of the population suffers from malnutrition. Nepal's life expectancy of 53 years and literacy rate of 26 percent remain among the lowest in the world.

For generations, only a footpath connected Gurung Gaon with the rest of the world. A recently built road (*left*) brought new conveniences and new problems. House sites were lost and fields suffered serious erosion damage during construction. Income sources also eroded. Passersby used to stop to rest and buy tea. Now, with the new road, stopping is not necessary.

Another important income source—collecting firewood—was lost when the nearby forest was recently declared a wildlife reserve. For the people of Gurung Gaon, hope for the future hinges on fast-growing trees for fodder, fencing and firewood and animals provided by Heifer Project (*following pages*).

"The women of Gurung Gaon were in a very dark place. Now, because of Heifer Project, they see the light of day."

Nirmala Gurung *(near left)*
Former Women's Group Chairperson

BUFFALO FOR SALE   In 1995, 39 families of Gurung Gaon village received a dairy buffalo *(above left)* from Heifer Project. The buffalo were a direct response to a request from a women's group organized to promote community improvement. The group wanted buffalo because unlike cows, which are sacred to Hindus, the male offspring of dairy buffalo can be sold at market.

"Economic benefits from the animals have come slowly," says Dr. Mahendra Lohani, director of HPI/Nepal. "In the first two years, 40 percent of the buffalo calved and were producing milk." Villagers thus continue to rely on HPI goats for sustenance and income *(left)*. Young animals are kept in the family kitchen *(right)* to protect them from jackals, bears and other wild predators living in the nearby forest.

"There have been many spiritual changes," says Nirmala Gurung *(above)*, past chairperson of the women's group. "As we have worked together to improve our situation, the love and affection we have for each other have grown tremendously."

The women's group started a savings fund to be used during times of need, with each person contributing 30 cents a month. These funds have been used for medical treatment, home improvements and food.

"HPI encourages us to do more for ourselves," says Nirmala.

CAMBODIA

Heifer Project and other development organizations have found it difficult to establish a strong presence in Cambodia, and for good reason. War, civil strife and genocide sparked by the 1970s madness of the late dictator Pol Pot have left a quarter of the population dead, the government in turmoil and a previously rich agrarian society in shambles.

At Cheung-Ek, one of the "killing field" sites, a glass pagoda housing hundreds of skulls stands as a stark reminder of the country's recent horrors (near right). The mass graves from which the skulls were exhumed lie only a few feet away, and the smell of death still lingers.

"Ninety percent of the intellectuals were killed by the Khmer Rouge," says Dr. Sen Sovann, HPI representative and dean of the Royal University of Agriculture. "I feel lucky to have survived, but unlucky to be born in Cambodia."

VACCINE IN ACTION Water buffalo play a part in rebuilding shattered lives and villages and are instrumental in reestablishing the nation's rice production. Since 1986, Heifer Project has helped develop and fund the country's only laboratory to produce vaccine combating *Hemorrhagic Septicemia*, a major killer of water buffalo and cattle in southeast Asia.

Housed in an 8-by-16-foot trailer and forced to work on the floor for lack of counter space, technicians (*left*) overcome trying conditions to produce an incredible 600,000 doses annually. At 14 cents a dose, the medication is cheap insurance for an animal that can easily cost the average Cambodian family several years of wages.

Managing a smile despite her fearfulness, the girl photographed with her family's water buffalo (*above*) would not give her name. Parents warn their children against talking with strangers; people still disappear in the unsettled countryside.

VIETNAM

Nguyen Thi Hai (*near right*) knows the secret behind her Yorkshire pigs' affection: they'll do anything—including pose for pictures—for a banana. Although the pigs are only one month old, she and other family members have already invested considerable time with them, including sleeping near the brood so they will not be stolen.

Hai, an HPI project farmer, lives along the maze of waterways and canals comprising the lower Mekong River Delta. Since 1992, when 31 families received Yorkshire pigs, her project has passed on pigs to more than 150 new members. An additional 800 area families also raise the same breed, having purchased them from project members.

Heifer Project began work in Vietnam's Mekong Delta in 1986 with the University of Can Tho School of Veterinary Medicine. Known as South Vietnam's "rice bowl," the Delta was once the richest and most populated portion of the country. Today, the area's productivity is far below that of prewar days.

Having received HPI pigs in July 1994, Nguyen Van Trang (*far right, in blue boat*) now finds his family beating the income averages. He has used profits from selling his pigs to buy a boat, television and a refrigerator.

"The old boat used oars and didn't have a motor," he says. "The new boat is good for my health because it conserves energy and time." He uses it to take his children to school and to transport pigs to market.

COMMUTING TO WORK   Job satisfaction is mission number one for the 330-pound Yorkshire breeding boar known as B1 *(near left)*. Whenever the gate of his pen swings open, he willingly climbs aboard the small river boat and into his cage because, as owner Nguyen Van Dung says, "He knows he's going to be happy."

Because of B1's abundant offspring (including the pigs on the preceding pages), knowledge of his prowess has spread throughout the lower Mekong. Yorkshire pigs are popular among Vietnamese farmers because they produce large healthy litters, put on weight faster than local breeds, and command top dollar at the market.

Bustling with activity shortly after sunrise, Can Tho Market on the Cai Rang River *(far left)* typifies the floating markets that congregate most mornings in the lower Mekong Delta. HPI farmers use small boats to bring pigs, ducks and produce to these waterborne shopping centers, where they are sold to buyers in larger boats who will transport their goods as far as Ho Chi Minh City.

"HPI emphasizes spirit and friendship. It's like one big family working together. Other organizations only focus on efficient use of money. They forget about the importance of love and spirit."

Dr. Chau Ba Lôc *(far right)*
Director, HPI/Vietnam

HELPING HANDS   At the Can Tho School for Handicapped Children, teacher Dinh Van Ut gently guides Huynh Nhat Oanh, a blind student, through the process of feeding the institution's pigs *(near right)*.

The school, located south of Ho Chi Minh City, specializes in teaching blind and deaf students marketable job skills. The Vietnamese government and several private international organizations lent financial support to the school, while Heifer Project supplied training, swine and poultry.

Dr. Chau Ba Lôc, director of HPI/Vietnam, began working with the Can Tho Red Cross Society Nursing Home for Elderly People and Orphans in 1993 *(far right)*. Heifer Project began supporting the home, which houses around 60 elderly people and 40 orphans with chickens, pigs and goats. The children help care for the animals and deliver food to seniors unable to walk.

THAILAND

> *"Every country is like a garden. If the Akha don't accept change and get education, they will be like a weed in the garden."*

Yote Kukaewkasem
Director, Development, Agricultural and
Educational Project for Akha (DAPA)

Unchanged for centuries, the Akha people of northern Thailand and Myanmar (Burma) have led a quiet existence. They live on isolated mountaintops in bamboo houses, raising livestock and cultivating crops—all in strict accordance with ancient rituals and traditions they call the "Akha Way" *(far left)*.

Within the last decade, the government's opium and poppy eradication program brought roads and electricity into remote areas. The Akha suddenly find themselves slapped in the face by the modern age. Heifer Project realized that if the Akha are to survive in this new world, they must be enabled to meet these challenges head-on. With an estimated 70 percent of the Akha illiterate, children's education is crucial to their ability to adapt. Heifer Project training and animals are providing families with the income necessary to educate the next generation.

With his HPI water buffalo, farmer Asuh Chermur *(near left, red cap)* can cultivate four times the amount of land he could by hand. He faithfully cools his buffalo twice daily, at midday and again in the evening.

As with most Akha who have never been officially recognized as citizens by the Thai government, legally, Asuh owns no other property besides his animals.

FACES OF CHANGE   Quick to adopt western ways, students at the HPI-supported Saen Suk Akha Hostel in northern Thailand *(right and above)* spend 10 months of the year living at the hostel while attending government schools. Since most Akha villages do not have a school, students must pursue their education in town schools.

At the hostel, students enjoy better food and more social life than in their home villages, while becoming fluent in the Thai language. Their two months of "vacation" at home are spent speaking only the tribal language as they labor beside their parents in the fields.

The Development, Agricultural and Educational Project for Akha (DAPA) of the Lahu Baptist Convention has established three such hostels in northern Thailand. Originally founded to improve the quality of life and preserve the culture of the Akha people, DAPA involves tribal elders in hostel activities.

"We believe that ancient traditions and modern education can live in harmony," says HPI/Thailand Director Niwatchai Suknaphasawat.

REVOLVING FUND   Heifer Project's support of DAPA began in 1987, when it set up a revolving fund program—mostly providing three-year, zero-interest loans—to help the Akha purchase buffalo, cattle, pigs and to offer critical training in their care.

The girls at Saen Suk help prepare every meal (*far left*), while the boys care for the hostel's HPI pigs (*near left and below*). A crossbreed between Chinese and Thai stock, pigs from Heifer Project fatten to market weight in half the time of local breeds and offer a higher quality of meat.

"I cannot stand by myself in a heavy wind," says Yote Kukaewkasem, DAPA director. "HPI has been a good partner. Through the animals, it has provided the Akha with better food and money for their children's education."

SOUTH KOREA

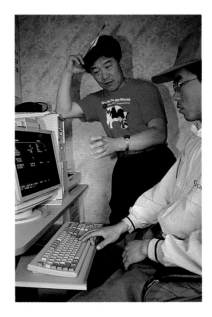

Mechanized, westernized and wired, HPI projects in South Korea contrast dramatically with most of those in the rest of Asia. Since the end of the Korean War, South Koreans have built one of the fastest growing economies in the world. Its per capita gross national product mushroomed from about $60 in 1953 to more than $10,000 in 1996. But when HPI assistance began before the end of the war, thoughts were not on prosperity but on survival; people were desperately hungry, some reduced to eating tree bark.

Eung-Kyu Min received an HPI heifer in 1963. Since then, he, his wife and son have grown their small farm into a fully mechanized dairy operation, milking 63 Holstein cows twice daily (*far right*). It used to take about 15 minutes to milk each cow by hand, but thanks to the sophisticated equipment, several animals can now be milked at once in only a few minutes.

Yun-sok Choe and Han Young, shown discussing computerized milk production records (*near right, upper*), represent second and third generation HPI involvement. Choe, a recent university graduate, returned to run his family's dairy farm after his father, an early project partner, retired. Han Young continues his family's tradition as an HPI volunteer: his grandfather helped initiate HPI programs in southern South Korea.

These families and others belong to an HPI group well known for generosity. Im-O Chong (*near right, lower*) used profits from his dairy to purchase land for his church. In the past decade, 25 members have raised money to buy animals and provide training in China and Thailand. They recently collected an additional $6,000 to support HPI's work in famine-stricken North Korea.

"We used to be very hungry and poor," says Eung-Kyu Min. "Now we are rich and give to other people. It's our Christian duty and the spirit of HPI."

I n the "new" Europe, poverty is widespread and income has declined for many. But Heifer Project has a unique mission in the countries ruled by communism until a decade ago. The aim is to assist in the transition from state dominated, centrally planned economic systems, to private, market-oriented, small-scale agriculture.

As captured in the pictures that follow, life in Central and Eastern Europe again revolves around the family. People who were not allowed to farm for themselves for more than a generation are now rediscovering the farming techniques their parents were forced to forget. Along with this has come a rekindling of traditional crafts and the heritage of helping each other and deciding for oneself.

The transition is not an easy one. Unemployment has soared as inefficient state industries have closed. There is no more glut of government jobs, and much of the social safety net has disappeared. Heifer Project is in the middle of this transition—creating new jobs and increasing income; introducing better breeds and preserving the best of the old; building democracy from the community up.

Heifer Project introduces communities to a new development model. It's a change that can be as challenging as the situation in Europe that originally gave birth to Heifer Project in 1944. HPI founder Dan West was doling out milk powder in war-torn Spain in a futile effort to stem hunger and thought, "There must be a better way."

Ten-year old Gampe Vasile *(left)* looking out of a window in Vadu Izei, Romania, is an appropriate image of the new Eastern Europe framed by tradition. It is a Europe full of hope and energy, as well as one full of questions and struggle. Will the transition bring a better life for all, or will it cause further pockets of poverty and despair like that of the Roma (Gypsies) in Slovakia? Will the traditional skills that communism could not kill, such as stacking hay, making *piroges* and stitching dresses, survive capitalism? What will this generation pass on to the next?

Dr. James DeVries
Director, International Programs

CENTRAL/EASTERN
EUROPE

55

POLAND

After four decades of communist rule, newfound freedom has brought economic hardship as Poland and other Eastern European nations struggle with the transition to a free market economy. Most of the out-dated and inefficient state-run factories and farms have already closed. The resulting high unemployment has forced many to go back to their roots—the small family farm *(far left)*.

The average farm in southeastern Poland is around seven acres, with two cows and a few pigs. About half the families own horses *(left)*, which are safer than tractors for working the hilly terrain.

With the help of Rotary International and the Mellon Foundation, Heifer Project established pilot projects in rabbit and goat production as well as the genetic preservation of Simmental and Polish Red cattle.

"The greatest challenge is to encourage people to think and act for themselves," says Jerry Aaker, Heifer Project's director of training. "The government used to take care of everything and discouraged the people from asking questions."

"Don't be fooled by the large homes. As many as 20 family members live in each one, and they have many needs. Under the communists, homes were the only safe investment—they could not be confiscated like land. Houses were like a savings account to these people."

Anna Zawada
Former Director, HPI Central/Eastern Europe

"We work for our children, not ourselves. It's like a mission. We must take care and protect the children, so our grandchildren's lives will be easier."

**Bernardyna Suwala,
HPI Farmer**

NO GENERATION GAP   Three generations living under one roof—like the Jozef Suwala family pictured here—is the tradition in many villages of Eastern Europe. Jozef (*left*), who received a Simmental cow from Heifer Project a few years ago, is project chairman for Mymlon village in southeastern Poland.

He and his wife, Bernardyna (*below*), live on a small farm with their two adult sons, a daughter-in-law and four grandchildren. The family shares work on the farm and finds living together much more economical than if each son built his own house and barn. The house is set up like a small apartment building, with the family cooking together in the main kitchen (*far left*).

MILK RUN   Zbyszek Gierlicki's early-morning milk run grows progressively longer as more and more area farmers like the Jozef Suwala family (*above and previous pages*) obtain high production dairy cattle.

Hitching horse to wagon at first light, Gierlicki clomps his way along village alleys and country roads picking up cans of fresh milk from about 15 neighboring farms—a process that seems more pleasure than chore to a passenger accustomed to life in a faster lane. Upon arrival at the dairy collection station, the pace quickens as his cans are methodically unloaded and the milk is measured, tested for quality and transferred to storage vats (*right*).

Once transferred back to his narrow wagon, the lightened containers bang and clatter as Gierlicki retraces his route, keeping his horse's pace steady as he unloads each farm's cans.

"The children want to forget about their childhood and bad experiences. So they paint happy things— flowers, nature scenes, houses. They paint their dreams."

Jan Nowak
Vice Director, Debinki Orphanage

JUST A FACADE   The elegant exterior of the structure housing the Debinki Orphanage outside Warsaw *(far right)* is but a facade. Closer inspection of this once-grand mansion reveals years of neglect. Like most large homes and major landhold-ings, the property was confiscated by the communist government after World War II and deteriorated badly.

Many of the young lives it shelters are also shells. Children come to this under-funded orphanage from backgrounds of harm and neglect at the hands of alcoholic or abusive parents.

Despite its somber mission, Debinki is in the process of developing a lively group of dedicated young artists, thanks to the efforts of Vice Director Jan Nowak *(near right)*. The children practice on discarded pieces of fiberboard using paint purchased with money earned from selling Polish pigs supplied by Heifer Project. The pigs are tended by the orphans, instilling in them a sense of responsibility and self-esteem.

"For these children who've suffered so much," says Nowak, "art is therapy."

ENDANGERED BREED   Polish Reds *(left)*, the only cattle breed native to Poland, once comprised most of the country's bovine population. Now they are in danger of becoming extinct. In the 1960s the government encouraged dairy farmers to switch to Holsteins, a breed that eventually proved unsuitable to southern Poland's climate because of problems with skin and hoof diseases.

With their smaller size and sharp hooves, Polish Red cattle are well-suited to mountainous conditions. They are remarkably disease resistant, thrive on low-quality fodder and are long-lived, with some cows remaining fertile to the age of 20.

HPI recipient Marek Kozka *(left)* is the son-in-law of Tadevz Janiczek, who has won numerous medals *(below)* for his work to improve Polish Red genetics. A few years ago, Tadevz teamed with local parish priest Antoni Poreba *(right)*, Heifer Project and local farmers to help reestablish a purebred herd in their 800-year-old village of Zegocina.

"It's important to preserve the biology so we don't lose the combination of genes," says Dr. Henryk Jasiorowski, director of HPI/Poland. "Once lost, they are lost forever for the whole of humanity."

"Many people have promised things, but HPI fulfilled its promise. So there is trust."

Antoni Poreba *(above)*
Parish Priest and President, Zegocina Dairy Cooperative

SLOVAKIA

Abused, despised and rejected, Gypsies have suffered unrelenting discrimination since migrating to Central and Eastern Europe from India more than 700 years ago. Some 20 million strong, Gypsies—or Roma people, as they prefer to be called—comprise Europe's largest minority, and about 10 percent of Slovakia's population.

During communist rule, Romas typically did the lowest forms of work, like cleaning streets. Now, the Romani families living in a settlement on the outskirts of Svinia (*left*) have 100 percent unemployment. Only one of the camp's 600 residents has ever been to high school.

A small river running through the village serves as bath and laundry, as well as the source of drinking water. There appears to be no provision made for food storage or waste disposal.

"The Slovak people see the Gypsies as parasites, claiming they steal their chickens and potatoes," says cultural anthropologist Alexander Mushinka. "They are definitely different, but we must build their social status and give them hope for a better future if there is to be meaningful change."

Heifer Project is teaming with Habitat for Humanity and other agencies to design a project that would provide the Svinia settlement with livestock, houses and jobs. Such lofty goals will require careful planning, execution and follow-up if the project is to have lasting significance.

ROMANIA

The beauty of the healthy Red Spotted cattle grazing above the village of Bologa in northwestern Romania *(far right)* makes it easier to understand a compliment traditionally given to local girls *(near right)*—"You are as pretty as your cow" (meaning a little plump).

Though it's hard to imagine, this traditional breed, referred to as Simmental except in Romania, recently faced extinction in Eastern Europe. Herd losses due to World War II, combined with a communist policy favoring Holsteins for the government's large dairies, caused a serious decline in the breed. The few remaining Red Spotted cattle faced the slaughterhouse as state farms went bankrupt after the end of communism.

Recognizing opportunity in adversity, Heifer Project organized its first multinational program to support the breed and improve its genetics. Project members from Poland, Slovakia, Ukraine and Romania now work closely together exchanging ideas and experiences involving Red Spotteds. A semen exchange program between the countries is in the works.

"It took us over a year to prepare for our cows," says Potra Gheorghe, Bologa's project leader. "Half the village laughed. 'Where are your cows from the Americans?' they would ask. Now they ask for pass-on animals of their own."

GRANDMA KNOWS BEST With snow on the ground six months of the year and winter temperatures that regularly plunge below zero, northeast Romania's mountain climate is too severe for growing grain. Since commercial feed is prohibitively expensive, a successful hay crop is critical to feed area livestock.

During the fall, Potra Gheorghe's horse Stella (*near left*) works from dawn to dark hauling hay from the fields surrounding Bologa village. Potra, HPI's project leader in Bologa, purchased the horse with his own funds specifically to share it with other project members. Now that small farms are reforming the economic backbone of Eastern Europe, horses are once again considered a valuable asset.

Around the remote village of Dorna Candrenilor nestled deep in the Carpathian Mountains, the art of stacking hay has remained unchanged for 300 years (*far left*). Shaping the stack for proper settling requires skill. So the task falls into the hands of the most experienced family member, in this case, the grandmother.

The final crucial step, placing a woven "ring" around the center pole, allows the grass to breathe yet prevents rain from penetrating the center of the stack.

"During communist rule, tractors were favored on the large state-run farms. Nearly half of the country's horses—over 600,000— were killed and fed to pigs."

Dr. Ovidiu Spinu
Director, HPI/Romania

> "During communism we were all the same—same house, same car, same bicycle. Now, it is better for some, worse for others, and some people are suspicious and jealous. Our goal is to preserve our traditions—as well as our community spirit."
>
> **Borlean Ion** *(below right)*
> **President, Fundatia Turistica**
> **Agro-Tur O.S.R.**

CRAFTING A FUTURE   Using soft, delicate strokes, Borlean Ion carefully brushes paint on glass *(right)* to depict colorful religious figures and symbols, a regional art form practiced in this part of northeastern Romania since the 1700s. His home village, Vadu Izei, enjoys a rising reputation among European tourists for its unspoiled natural beauty and concentration of traditional artists and craftsmen. But as president of the village committee for tourism and development, Ion's vision must be pragmatic as well as artistic.

During the long, harsh winter months, tourism to Vadu Izei plummets with the temperature. Residents like Cornisean Ileana *(above right)* are looking to a recently approved HPI dairy cow project to supply much needed income during the slow season. The fragrance of hand-sawed lumber surrounds Ileana as she stands in front of her barn, recently built to house a new HPI cow, one of 30 Swiss Brown cattle scheduled to be shipped to her village.

No one is more deeply committed to the long-term success of the project than its leader, Gampe Claudia. Laid off as a government veterinarian in 1997, she, along with husband Dumitru, is laying 4,000 bricks to create a cheese "factory" *(left)*. Claudia designed the building to process milk from HPI cattle into cheese.

LATIN AMERICA/ CARIBBEAN

S ince the 1950s, Heifer Project has provided thousands of living loans in the form of livestock to Latin American farm families to help them start a new life as land reform and other social changes come into play. The following photographs and text about Bolivia, Peru, and Guatemala are representative of HPI's program to build a just and sustainable world.

Centuries ago, when the Spanish settled the Americas, they found distinctive cultures, music, art and indigenous flora and fauna. Alpacas, llamas *(left)* and guinea pigs, domesticated since the last Ice Age, were nearly eliminated by the Spanish once they discovered the animals' religious significance among the Andean population. Indigenous people everywhere were forced into serfdom on *haciendas*, or large farms. They were not permitted to own land, seek education, speak Spanish, form unions or vote in elections. It was not until the 20th century that the hacienda system was abolished either through civil wars or democratic reforms.

Today, the HPI Latin America/Caribbean Program is a leader in supporting small-farm, family-based grassroots organizations that promote environmentally sound animal projects for food and income. HPI values the use of indigenous species, as well as local knowledge and skills. It provides education in a wide variety of critical areas including livestock management and soil and water conservation.

Training for both men and women is also a strong component in any project. It is done in a hands-on and gender-sensitive manner, providing skills necessary for everyone to reach his or her full potential.

Heifer Project works hand in hand with a number of local, national and international organizations to promote the dignity inherent in Central and South American people who are a unique blend of ethnic groups, Spanish history, technology and a love of the land.

Jim Hoey
Program Director, Latin America/Caribbean

BOLIVIA

With only clouds for company, an Aymara man keeps his herd of alpacas on the move *(far left)* as they graze high above his home village of Inca Katurapi. Domesticated more than 5,000 years ago, alpacas are ideally suited to the delicate Andean ecosystem. Their padded hooves do not damage soil structure and, unlike sheep, they clip grass with their teeth rather than pulling it up by the roots.

Like the animals they tend, the Aymara people are survivors. Conquered by the Incas in the 1400s, they were later dominated by the Spanish who used them as serfs under the hacienda land system. Despite past adversities, they have managed to retain their language and culture, including the tradition of sharing communal property and working together toward common goals.

This herd began in 1989 with 42 alpacas, a pass-on gift from Heifer Project working in conjunction with the Methodist Rural Development Program in Bolivia. Now numbering more than 175, the animals are communally owned—as are the alpine pastures on which they graze. Care of the alpacas rotates among 45 participating co-op families of Inca Katurapi, each overseeing the herd for a two-week stretch.

The growing herd provides villagers with valuable alpaca fleece and additional dietary protein. The animals also supply each family in the cooperative with 1,000 pounds of manure a year to spread on their fields and use as fuel.

An extensionist *(near left)* from the Methodist Church provides training in the herd's care and monitors the alpacas to see they stay healthy.

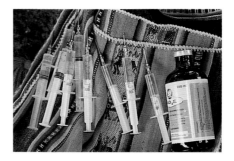

RAREFIED RODEO   Unlike its sometimes ill-tempered cousin, the llama, the alpaca is usually docile and good-natured—until the needles and syringes come out and the animals are rounded up for their annual treatment against intestinal worms and insects *(left and above)*.

The Aymara women do most of the dirty work, summarily wrestling each animal to the ground and keeping it pinned during the injections, while dodging mouthfuls of foul-smelling green cud the alpacas spit at them in protest. Following the shots, a blue mark painted on the head makes sure an animal will not be treated more than once.

This livestock health program resulted from HPI training that stresses the concept of "preventive maintenance." Proper nutrition and treatment against routine pests like fleas and mites all contribute to keeping livestock healthy at a minimal cost.

"These people are special. They don't work together just for economic benefit—it's deeper than that. They have a strong cultural identity and deep spiritual roots. They believe in getting outside themselves and serving one another to work out problems."

Gregorio Calle
Coordinator, Methodist Rural
Development Program in Bolivia

SHEARING TEAM   After the alpacas have been injected (*preceding pages*), hand-shearing with clippers requires another group effort (*near right*) and roughly one hour's time for each animal as up to eight pounds of fleece are removed.

Women weave the alpaca fiber into shawls and sweaters for their families and to sell at the market. Sale proceeds pay medical expenses and support an emergency loan fund available to co-op members.

NO IDLE HANDS   Passing on the tradition, a mother spins alpaca wool while overseeing the herd (*near left*). Idle hands are not a problem for the hard-working women of Inca Katurapi, whose daughters learn early in life that the group's success depends on each individual's effort.

With support from Heifer Project and the Evangelical Methodist Church of Bolivia, villagers continue to upgrade their skills in caring for their animals, fertilizing their fields with manure, and marketing the soft alpaca fiber. The alpaca herd is especially important because it adds a much needed economic diversity to this community that traditionally produces potatoes.

Because of Inca Katurapi's success with the herd and ability to work together, governmental and other organizations are now willing to lend them money. With this economic assistance, the villagers plan to grow their herd to 500 animals, a number they have determined will not overwhelm the fragile alpine vegetation.

VALUABLE PROTEIN   Sheep graze near the village of Inca Katurapi (*left*), three miles distant and 2,000 feet below the alpaca pastures. Land at this lower elevation is reserved for agriculture and livestock not adapted to high altitudes.

For centuries, guinea pigs have been a valuable protein supplement in the Aymaras' battle against malnutrition. Most families in this village own 20 to 40 of the animals, many of them a larger, improved variety provided by Heifer Project.

Training in guinea pig care has increased productivity and remedied problems with inbreeding. Once a year the village prepares a "community bath" of mild insecticide in which the animals are dipped to kill disease-carrying fleas (*above*).

The Aymara believe plants, animals, and people are interdependent. They carefully collect guinea pig manure and spread it on their fields; fat from the animals is applied as an ointment for sore muscles; the blood is used to bless the earth.

GUATEMALA

T his is macho land," says HPI/Guatemala field technician, Jonathån Guzmån. "Women and girls take care of household chores. Men and boys work in the fields."

For women in the parched highlands of eastern Guatemala, this means endless hours of hard physical labor, starting before daylight and lasting well past sunset. Simply providing enough water for their family and animals requires up to 10 trips daily to the nearest faucet along the government pipeline, balancing 20 pound jugs on their heads *(right)*. With rare exceptions, children like these girls quit school after the sixth grade to help their parents.

Families migrated to this remote area beginning in 1983, after the worst fighting of Guatemala's prolonged civil war was over. They came to buy small, hillside plots of some of this Central American nation's least productive and thus cheapest land—all they could afford. They were determined that no matter how arid and rocky it was, they would work the land as owners, not as tenants for the wealthy few who own most of the productive farmland.

"There were no goats in this area before HPI," says project president Feliciano Orellana. "Only a few cows. At first we wanted more cows. But we learned that a productive dairy cow can drink 18 gallons of water each day—a goat usually needs only one. And goats reproduce faster, need less food, and women and children can easily handle them *(following pages)*."

"I started with one goat. Now it's many things—land, new roof, corn grinder, electricity and water hose."

Francisca Sucite *(right)*
HPI Farmer

HOURS SAVED   As she has done almost every day since age eight, 79-year-old Francisca Sucite prepares fresh tortillas by hand *(near right)*. She crushes pieces of dried corn with a stone, then adds water. This mixture is further stone-ground into a fine paste, shaped into patties and cooked—a process unchanged since Mayan times more than 500 years ago.

Francisca's lifestyle mirrors that of most Guatemalan Indian women, but with a few notable improvements. With income from selling goats and cheese, Francisca recently purchased a manual corn grinder, saving her about two hours of labor daily. Even so, preparing meals for her extended family still demands six hours of her time each day.

Thanks to her Heifer Project goats acquired in 1990, Francisca can now afford newly available luxuries, including a plastic hose to tap water from the government spigot. This simple item saves her countless trips balancing a heavy water pot on her head.

Housing the goats in a raised pen *(far right)* protects them from theft and predators, simplifies manure collection and lets Francisca control their diet. When asked what the goats have meant to her, her eyes well with tears as she replies, "They give me my life."

PERU

Children coax a reluctant kite to fly *(right)* in Cajamarquilla, one of the growing number of shantytowns encircling Lima, Peru's capital and largest city.

About three million people live in these improvised communities, most without running water or electricity. Called "invaders" by the locals for their habit of showing up in the middle of the night, planting a flag and claiming some barren plot of land as their own, these newcomers first erect temporary shelters of straw or plastic. If they are lucky and find a source of income, they then build more permanent structures of brick and concrete.

Heifer Project has started with a small presence in Cajamarquilla, using guinea pigs and earthworms *(following pages)*. Once HPI determines what will work best, the projects will be expanded to better help the community work toward long-term success.

Urban migration spawned by rural poverty and terrorism couples with high unemployment to present huge problems for Peruvians recovering from decades of chaos. They have survived soaring inflation brought on by land reform, nationalization of industry in the '70s and terrorism from the murderous guerrilla movement, Shining Path, between 1980 and 1993.

The nation is rebuilding, but Lima strains with too many poor people.

SECRET WEAPON   "My dream is one house, one tree, and a better environment for every family," says HPI project worker Carlos Ccahuana *(right, in red cap)*. Simple sounding, it's a goal not easily achieved in Cajamarquilla, where a source of income is as rare as rain.

Carlos works with Rafael Albinagorta's family to improve their modest garden. For Rafael's family, the house has become a reality after five years of hard work, but the tree remains a dream. With unproductive soil and unreliable rainfall, plant life survives only with constant effort and precious water brought in by tanker truck and hand-carried to each home.

But Rafael has a secret weapon in his battle with nature—earthworms supplied by Heifer Project *(above)*. With Carlos' help, Rafael's "flock" of worms thrives in rich humus created by composting garbage. Producing an extraordinary amount of castings for their size, the worms have greatly improved the quality of soil in his garden. This simple organic process is environmentally sound and costs almost nothing.

COMPACT NUTRITION   Dionisia Llancari (*left*) is one of 17 HPI guinea pig project members in Cajamarquilla. Packing a surprising amount of nutritional punch in a small package, guinea pigs provide an ideal food source for people of limited means. With more protein and less cholesterol than beef, they reproduce quickly, require little care and are considered delicious by Peruvians.

At HPI's Lima office, staff members practice what they preach in the field, raising earthworms and guinea pigs on a small back porch. Like the villagers they assist, they try to recycle whenever possible, making creative use of discarded material.

With this attitude in mind, Carlos Ccahuana designed a planting rack (*above*) for growing guinea pig fodder in urban settings where land and water are limited. Built from lumber scraps and trays cut from used plastic containers, wire screen shelves are layered one above the other. Water percolates down to the bottom shelf, resulting in little to no waste.

Once his design is perfected, Carlos will share it with HPI guinea pig farmers.

"If the antidote had not been given this morning, the animals would have been dead by afternoon."

José Zapa Navarro
Paraveterinarian

LIFE ON THE EDGE   Sadly, three local cows in the village of Hunancan *(far left)* were mistakenly given an insecticide overdose. With only a few hours to spare, local paraveterinarian José Zapa Navarro administers life-saving intravenous medication to one of the overdosed cows *(near left)*.

Livestock are a valuable commodity in the tiny settlement, perched above an irrigated river valley running through the desert coast of central Peru. "It's a big loss if even one cow dies," explains Navarro. "Each of the three affected animals represents about 30 percent of its owner's net worth."

Since 1986, when they first arrived to look for temporary work, life has been a struggle for the seven families of Hunancan, battling terrorists and thieves as well as the parched climate. For two years, they worked every day digging a canal to divert river water to a strip of valley land where they planted income-producing fruit trees and row crops.

Besides supplying the families with guinea pigs, Heifer Project is helping to educate the people about the use of manure as fertilizer and the value and dangers of pesticides and other chemicals.

TRANSFORMING THE DESERT   With military-like precision, tree planters from Loma Negra village in northern Peru (*far right*) advance eight steps, dig in their heels and drop three or four algarroba seeds in the depressions—a process that will be repeated for more than a mile.

Members of the mesquite family, mature algarroba trees can produce an incredible three tons of sugar-rich seed pods per acre, useful as livestock feed and for the production of a coffee-like drink (*following pages*).

With seed donated by Heifer Project (*above*), the group hopes to transform this barren stretch of land into an orchard of nutrient-rich algarroba trees. All their hopes hinge on the El Niño weather phenomenon bringing needed rain to sprout the seeds, as it did to a nearby area planted before the 1983 rains (*near right*).

The planting line must be organized so that each seedling can grow without competition from its neighbors. Plastic bottles will protect the seedlings from grazing goats and lizards. A total of 8,000 seeds were planted this day on about 10 acres, with an anticipated survival rate of less than 50 percent.

*"This kitchen is their factory.
Their dreams are here."*

**Juan Flores
Director, HPI/Peru**

SMALL FACTORY, BIG PLANS   Members of the Eternal Help Mothers' Club process algarroba coffee in their community kitchen *(far right)*. Jump-started by a Heifer Project loan, 12 families are involved in this cooperative effort that began in 1997 with training at a local university.

Stored in an air-tight adobe shed for two or three months, seed pods from the algarroba tree turn a golden brown *(near right)*. Next, the pods are cleaned, broken into pieces and ground into a meal that is carefully browned on a stove. The final product retails for around two dollars a pound, has a honey-cinnamon fragrance, is non-caffeinated and tastes like—well, it has a flavor all its own.

"By storing the pods until August or September when the price is higher, these families are achieving a 25 to 30 percent increase in income per year," says Juan Flores, director of HPI/Peru.

THE LONG DROUGHT   Life has always been hard for the indigenous people of Loma Negra in northwestern Peru. For generations, simply maintaining a food supply in this unforgiving environment proved difficult, sometimes impossible. Significant change was unthinkable.

Enter HPI/Peru's volunteers—college graduates in animal husbandry who advise villagers how to upgrade their livestock, improve their family's nutrition and generate new sources of income. That's not an easy task in an area where the date and time of the last measurable precipitation is remembered by everyone—exactly five years, seven months, eleven days ago at 10:00 A.M.

Wilmer Demoche (*left, red cap*), an HPI volunteer, instructs members of the Loma Negra community in the care of recently acquired sheep. Several are a special crossbreed of tropical sheep specifically selected for the dry, hot climate.

Walter Valdivieso (*above, white hat*), also a volunteer, introduced a bee program to the villagers in 1997. The bees pollinate the crops, and each colony of 60,000 bees produces more than 60 pounds of honey a year to sweeten the community's food and income.

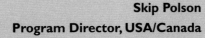

Heifer Project has worked in North America since 1947, providing support and encouragement to more than 250 local projects in 36 states and two provinces of Canada. Each of these projects was planned, designed and managed by local people to improve the quality of life for themselves, their families and their communities.

Despite the relative wealth we enjoy in North America, census bureau statistics reflect that poverty persists in 535 counties. These economically depressed pockets can be found across the breadth of the land, from Maine to California. And even though we have government welfare programs that prevent people from actually starving, many people languish without meaningful work and with little hope for the future.

Family farms were once the foundation of American life. Now, many small farms have been consolidated into large, corporate-owned agribusinesses. Rural communities wither as people move to the cities seeking a better life.

In spite of these difficulties, local people throughout North America are working to change this situation in their own communities, and HPI is proud to be in partnership with them. Heifer Project helps them create their own vision of the future through participatory, values-based visioning and planning and to empower them to pursue their goals through appropriate livestock and livestock-related enterprises.

In this collaboration, everyone learns how to work more effectively toward agricultural sustainability and how to nurture healthy, dynamic human communities. Heifer Project partners like Neil Hoffman (*left*) provide leadership in agricultural, economic and community development right where they live—which is where it matters most!

Skip Polson
Program Director, USA/Canada

UNITED STATES

Neil and Denise Hoffman (*right*) believe in living lightly on the earth. Having developed a 60-acre integrated farm in eastern Kentucky, they proudly count themselves among the less than 2 percent of Americans farming full-time.

The Hoffmans raise hogs, dairy goats, chickens, strawberries, shiitake mushrooms, blueberries, peppers and cabbage while keeping their root cellar well-stocked with a variety of garden produce (*far right*).

Crops and livestock complement each other on the Hoffmans' farm, and natural biological processes serve as an alternative to chemical pesticides. For example, bees produce honey and pollinate crops, hogs feed on ground cover between crop rotations and praying mantises are collected to help manage pests.

Several years ago, Heifer Project helped the Hoffmans procure some of their first animals—two sows and later, a few goats. Ever since, their role with HPI has been as givers rather than receivers. Living in one of the poorest counties in Kentucky where there is a high illiteracy rate, they have helped other project members with their record-keeping.

"The key to true sustainable agriculture is learning to work with nature, rather than clobbering her with science."

Neil Hoffman *(far left)*
HPI Farmer

CLOSE QUARTERS   Wendy Wilmot still remembers the premonition she felt when first reading the classified ad—*For Sale: 70 acres with 20-acre field, off the road, no electricity.* "In my heart, I knew that this was it," she says. Living in Maine's remote Aroostook County where full-time jobs are scarce, she and her husband, Steve, had been searching for an affordable small farm for almost seven years without success.

Because of the rocky soil and short growing season, the Wilmots struggle to make ends meet. Steve takes temporary jobs whenever he can find them. Heifer Project's Northern Aroostook Homesteaders project helps by educating the Wilmots and other farmers on such rural skills as gardening, canning, making cheese, butter and crafts.

The Wilmots share their one-room, 300-square-foot cabin with children, David and Brittany, two dogs and three cats. Their small barn (*far right, upper*) allows body heat to accumulate, helping their animals, including an HPI Jersey cow, to survive winter temperatures that sometimes dip below -40°F. Insulated seats (*far right, below*) add comfort in the outhouse.

Wendy and Steve consider home schooling (*near right*) an integral part of their homesteading experience. "We like being active participants in their learning," says Wendy.

BIGGEST FAMILY MEMBER   Chris and Sue Caswell, along with children Christy, Rob and Erin, give their animals extra attention on their farm near Houlton, Maine *(right and above)*—especially their 1,600-pound draft horse, Prince.

"We got him in the fall of '96 with a loan from Heifer Project, and he's been a member of the family ever since," says Chris. "He loves peppermints and attention; everybody goes to check on him 10 times a day. You just can't realize the power and intelligence he has. It's almost a spiritual experience working with an animal like that."

For small-scale farmers like the Caswells, horsepower makes both economic and ecological sense. Prince runs on home-grown fuel, operates efficiently in winter conditions that would strand a tractor, and contributes an incredible 10 tons of fertilizer to the farm each year.

"We depend on him a lot," Chris says. "Our livelihood comes from wood—cutting firewood, a little for pulp. We use eight to twelve cords ourselves just to get through the winter. Except for my chain saw, when we go into the woods together, it's like stepping back 100 years."

"We need to build confidence in our young people, and karate does that. It teaches a positive point of view and the need to focus."

Ben Gamble
Project Leader

BUILDING A COMMUNITY   Ben Gamble *(left, in black)* trained in the martial arts in the U.S. Army. Now a substitute teacher, school bus driver and HPI project leader in central Alabama, he focuses on finding ways to convince young people in the rural Flatwood community to return home when they finish school.

"Our best natural resources are our children," he says. "We need to help them develop sources of income if they're going to stay in this area." One way is with HPI-sponsored "pastured poultry." A mobile pen is constructed *(right)* to protect the young birds and placed in an available area of pasture. Each day the pen is moved to provide a fresh spot that the birds will forage and fertilize.

The birds grow to market weight in eight weeks. Popular among knowledgeable consumers because of their tasty natural flavor, healthy pastured poultry can yield significant profits and improved pastures for their producers.

In line with Heifer Project's emphasis on community building, members have actively supported pastured poultry enterprises and other community efforts like the summer food program financed by the state and organized by the people of Flatwood *(above, far right)*. Some HPI project holders belong to the volunteer fire department of nearby Greene County *(above)* and also participate in the Greene County Farmers Self-Help Group.

MORE THAN MONEY   A spin-off from a grassroots movement to save the land from developers in northern New Mexico's Chama Valley, Tierra Wools has grown from modest beginnings into a blossoming hand-weaving workshop and retail store. Its worker-owners, mostly women, produce traditional and contemporary weavings in the Rio Grande style (*right*) using natural and hand-dyed yarn spun from locally grown sheep's wool (*above*).

Housed in a century-old mercantile store in the Hispanic community of Los Ojos, the business enjoys annual sales of $270,000. It employs around 30 people, several of whom belong to the local HPI cattle project. While weaving sales are brisk during the warm months, business at the store plunges in winter. Heifer Project animals bring some year-round income security. But according to Tierra Wools production manager Sophia Chavez, even the lean times are worth it.

"Tierra Wools is about much more than just making money," she says. "It's about people, families, tradition and cultures. We hope our success can stand as an example to rural communities everywhere."

"My family gets a chunk of income in the spring and fall from wool and lambs, but the rest of the year, I depend on my weaving and HPI calves."

Molly Manzanares
Los Ojos Project Member

"For me, butchering is the most spiritual part of my relationship with my animals. Not only am I responsible for their lives— but also their deaths."

Lorraine Vissering
Overlook Farm workshop

LEARNING RESPECT   "Animal husbandry goes beyond providing food and water," says June Baker as she strains to ear-tag a goat *(right)*. A project holder from New York, she and other HPI members are attending a fall agriculture and marketing workshop at Overlook Farm, Heifer Project's east coast education center near Rutland, Massachusetts. "It's a real nurturing relationship—an interdependence," Baker adds. "My animals depend on me; I depend on them. I put a lot of energy into caring for them—and I'm rewarded with their loyalty and affection."

The point of the gathering is to offer training to HPI members in livestock care, farm management and alternative farm enterprises, with the emphasis on inexpensive, low technology methods. During the weekend workshop, approximately 20 participants listen to presentations on a variety of topics, including cheese and butter making, working with draft horses *(left)*, milking and medicating goats and humanely butchering small animals *(above)*.

As a group, the participants are united in the sensitivity and care they express toward their animals. "Actually, I hate to use the word animal," says Katherine Gordon from Snowy River Farm in Vermont. "It doesn't elevate them to the level of respect they deserve."

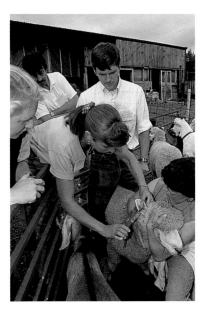

"The kids bring their muscles as well as their minds. They leave with smiles and sweat on their faces, increased global awareness and chigger bites."

**Mark Schnarr,
Director, Heifer Ranch**

THE HOME RANCH   Billing itself as a hands-on campus, the 1,200-acre Heifer Ranch near Perryville, Arkansas *(near left)*, hosts more than 20,000 visitors a year, while teaching solutions to world hunger through animal agriculture.

Activities include Elderhostel programs for seniors, Global Village for youth and a ropes course that develops teamwork in both elementary students and corporate managers.

Some 9,000 students explore the ranch on field trips each spring and fall. Week-long Service Learning Camps are conducted primarily for church youth groups. These young people supply energy and enthusiasm for ranch chores, maintaining farm roads and replacing the thatch roof of the Asia House *(below)*, while bunking in the "Heifer Hilton" barn *(far left)*.

S afari! This Swahili word meaning journey invokes images of East African wildlife and adventure. Kenya, Tanzania and Uganda, surrounding Lake Victoria—the headwaters of the Nile and Africa's largest lake—invite Westerners on safari to bring in vital foreign exchange. The second largest continent in the world, Africa has a wealth of natural beauty, history and cultural diversity. Discoveries in Tanzania by Louis and Mary Leakey show that people have lived there since the beginning of time. In Kenya alone there are 70 different tribal groups.

But most Africans will never experience the wonders of their continent. Their lives are fully occupied with the struggle to survive and to obtain basics like food, clothing, shelter and income. Colonialism has left Africans feeling abused, exploited or dependent. Lack of food and income, the AIDS epidemic and annual population growth rates more than 3 percent rob people of hope.

Heifer Project began assisting Africans after World War II, when a ship filled with livestock and HPI cowboys unloaded its ark-like cargo in Ethiopia. Today, the African continent houses HPI's largest program with longstanding projects in Kenya, Tanzania, Uganda, Cameroon and Zimbabwe, plus newer programs in Zambia, Mozambique, Ghana and South Africa. Many projects involve foraging, ruminant animals like cows, goats or camels (left). Projects with chickens or pigs, which can compete directly with humans for food, are added only where food such as corn or rice is in surplus.

Whenever possible, Heifer Project focuses on assisting women. In developing countries, women have not received an equitable amount of attention. Maternal mortality rates are higher in Africa than anywhere else in the world. In Tanzania, where 80 percent of the population lives in rural areas, surveys show that women spend at least three times as much time as men in transport activities, such as carrying water and firewood, and they transport four times as much in volume.

Heifer Project strives to listen to the voiceless. Living loans of livestock are a good place to start. The following pages will take you on a safari of African life outside the usual tourist haunts. You will feel the hope of HPI's journey to alleviate poverty and hunger.

Dan Gudahl
Program Director, Africa/Near East

117

TANZANIA

With vistas that seem to stretch forever, Tanzania contains some of Africa's most spectacular geography, including the Serengeti Plain and 19,340-foot-high Mount Kilimanjaro. Although the scenery appears limitless, natural resources are not.

Almost two-thirds of Tanzania is unsuitable for livestock because of tsetse-fly infestations or cannot be cultivated due to lack of rain. Women trek up to five miles daily to fetch water for their families and livestock. Most families grow barely enough food to survive.

Ever-increasing populations of people and livestock threaten precious grasslands. Communal pastures used by Maasai and Waarusha herders suffer from overgrazing and are infested with ticks and other parasites. Only half of school-age children attend school. Many, like this nine-year-old boy tending goats (*right*), are needed as herders.

Heifer Project requires a "zero-grazing" policy among most project holders in Tanzania and similar environmentally sensitive areas. Keeping livestock in pens of the proper size with provisions for food, water and exercise prevents overgrazing. It also permits efficient collection of manure and protects animals from disease. With fodder grown nearby and brought to the animals, crops are protected and children can attend school instead of watching the herd.

Heifer Project also encourages farmers to keep fewer but more productive cows; one crossbred cow can produce up to 15 times as much milk as a local cow.

THE TOLL OF EROSION   When rain does come to the high, arid plains of Tanzania, it falls in torrents during seasons known as the "long rains." Because of the fragile nature of the volcanic soil, hillside livestock trails quickly degrade into gullies *(near right)*.

To combat this problem, Heifer Project works with the Waarusha, traditional hunters and herders related to the Maasai. Relatively new to agriculture, the Waarusha have little understanding of sound farming practices and erosion control methods. Heifer Project reintroduced them to concepts of contour farming *(above)* once practiced by British colonialists, and recommended planting trees and grass on terraces to hold the soil and feed their livestock.

Heifer Project provides seeds to the Habari Maalum (Good News) Tree Planting Project nursery outside Arusha *(far right)*, which distributes more than 400,000 seedlings a year to area farmers. Fast-growing trees like the leucaena provide fodder and firewood as well as shade and nitrogen to keep soil fertile.

"Each year during the heavy rains, we lose up to seven tons of topsoil per acre."

Erwin Kinsey
Director, HPI/Tanzania

MODEL FARMER   Loti Sareyo Sandilen (*above*) received a quick lesson in soil erosion one night in 1988 when a driving rain washed 800 pounds of newly-planted Irish potatoes down to the bottom of his hillside field in mere minutes. He had spent his entire savings on this crop and was able to salvage only one-fourth of his investment.

With advice from soil conservationists, Loti and his wife Lightness reworked their field, building ridges and digging drainage ditches across the steep slope. Napier grass and leucaena trees planted on the contours helped to hold the soil while providing fodder for the family cows. At the end of the dry season, the Sandilens' crops of beans and corn thrived while their neighbors' withered from lack of compost and water absorption.

Heifer Project recognized the Sandilens' success by furnishing them with a pregnant heifer. Now Loti helps his neighbors implement soil conservation techniques, a prerequisite for them also to receive an HPI heifer.

Thanks to income from his high-yield crops and growing dairy herd, Loti has been able to build a permanent cement house for his family (*near right*).

BREAKING THE CYCLE A simple calf (*above*)—an HPI pass-on from a neighbor—was a gift beyond the wildest dreams of Michael Lema and his family (*near left*).

This animal represents more than four times the Lemas' previous annual income. But money is only one measure of the heifer's worth.

When she calves, the cow will provide fresh milk to the Lemas' two children, who are in desperate need of additional protein in their diets. There will be plenty of milk left over to sell and the cow's calf will be passed on to another family. A jump in the Lemas' income will lead to a more comfortable house, education for the children and an improved lifestyle.

In the subsistence economy of rural Tanzania, one calf possesses the power to break the cycle of poverty and give a family hope for a brighter future.

That is the animal's greatest value of all.

CAMELS OR CATTLE   Striking in appearance and long respected for their independent ways, the Maasai people of East Africa proudly cling to a nomadic life and culture that measures wealth by the number of cattle owned. Sandals made from recycled tires are a rare concession by some Maasai to the modern world *(below left)*.

However, this romanticized tribe and its animals are now endangered by droughts and land reforms that confine herds to ever-shrinking pastures. The Maasai desperately need alternatives and some are convinced that camels offer many advantages over cattle in a harsh, arid climate like theirs.

Camels produce more milk and require less water than local cows. Their padded feet, big as platters *(below right)*, leave little sign of their passing—unlike cows and other hoofed animals that can destroy grass and cause soil erosion when overgrazing occurs.

After completing a training period with an experimental group of 21 Heifer Project camels in remote northern Tanzania, Mary Kambaini *(left)* and other members of her project group are eager to assume full responsibility for the herd *(right and following pages)*.

*"Even when I die,
my children will know
that this animal belonged
to me."*

**Mary Kambaini
Project Member**

A NEW TRADITION   Illiterate like most Maasai women,
Mary Kambaini uses her fingerprints to sign Heifer Project's
camel contract *(near right and above)*. Since Mary is a widow, her
son cosigned the contract. Of her 14 children, he is one of only
four who still survive.

Once she completed the agreement, Mary became the sole
owner of an animal. That's still a rare event in Maasai society,
where men traditionally have owned all the property.

Before the camels were distributed, primary responsibility
for their care lay in the hands of trainer Paulo Okida *(far right)*.
Young and single, Paulo declined an opportunity to own a
camel. In the future, he hopes to choose a bride and begin his
herd with a pass-on camel.

UGANDA

ngela Kadoli (*near right*) makes it look easy to carry a heavy load on her three-mile walk to the local market outside of Mbale in eastern Uganda. In addition to a 10-pound baby tied to her waist, Angela's basket of tree-ripened bananas weighs about 55 pounds. But it is a weight she happily bears.

Her bananas are especially large and plentiful thanks to regular fertilization by manure from her mother's HPI dairy cow. The fruit should bring a good price at market—the equivalent of three dollars or so—which will be used to buy sugar and soap for her family.

With fertile soil and abundant rainfall (*far right*), bananas and other crops grow profusely in many parts of Uganda, dubbed "the pearl of Africa" a century ago by Winston Churchill. But during the last three decades, the pearl has lost its luster as civil war and disease have devastated the country. The war alone cost more than 800,000 lives and the AIDS epidemic has infected an estimated 20 percent of Uganda's adults.

So many men were killed in the fighting, that women now have added responsibilities. Children, orphaned by the war and AIDS, now live with extended families of aunts, uncles and grandparents, increasing pressure on already strained resources. Countless other orphans live as street children—part of another growing problem in Uganda.

*"Why I survived, I don't know.
I try to keep away from that memory.
I try as hard as I can."*

Elias Musanje *(far left)*
HPI Farmer

REBUILDING A LIFE   Memories come hard for Elias Musanje as he stands in front of his war-damaged house *(far left)* and recalls the terrible night in 1983 when eight family members were murdered. Family grave site are located near the home, a Ugandan tradition *(near left)*. They stand in mute testimony to the ravages of civil war and AIDS that have plagued the country.

In the 1980s, more than a million Ugandans abandoned their homes, seeking safety from violence. Elias fled deep into the countryside and—despite a college degree in glass technology—dug ditches to support his family. It was not smart to be known as an educated man, since troops often targeted such people.

Two years later when it was safe, Elias returned to what was left of his farm to rebuild his life. A dairy cow from Heifer Project gave him renewed hope for better times. As his herd grew, so did his income. He is now proud to say that he has six children in college, and he is weighing the difficult decision to sell part of his prized herd to gain the start-up capital for a small factory that will produce laboratory glassware.

"There were times it seemed that life was not worth living," Elias says. "But I realized it wasn't the end of the road, that I had to gather some courage and get to work. Without the animals, I don't know how I could have managed."

> *"Malnourished children tend not to have expressions. Their bodies may recover, but their minds are dull and damaged."*
>
> **Dr. Margaret Makuru**
> **Deputy Director, HPI/Uganda**

FACE OF HUNGER   Worldwide, more than one billion people are undernourished; 185 million of these are preschool children.

Although the excellent growing conditions of Uganda helped prevent mass starvation during its years of civil turmoil, nutrition remains woefully inadequate. Carbohydrates from foods like bananas keep the body alive. But adequate protein, critical for proper mental and physical development of children, is lacking.

A visitor might reasonably guess Esther Kasakye (*near right*) to be around seven months old. She is actually two years old. Her grandmother, Blandina Naahale, is a new HPI project member. Blandina has planted pastures, built a pen and learned how to care for a pass-on heifer to be delivered in one month. The cow's milk will supply critically needed protein for Esther.

Though her physical recovery is expected to be relatively swift, the prognosis for Esther's long-term mental condition is less certain.

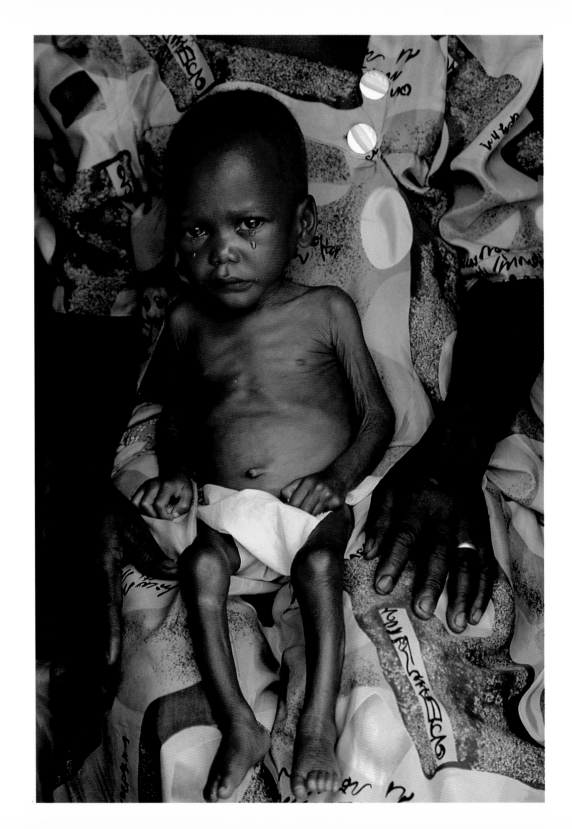

A Sad Cycle Though the outward signs of malnutrition are subtle, its impact on children can be devastating. Puffy cheeks, swollen bellies, thinning, light-colored hair and expressionless faces *(near left)*, indicate a serious lack of dietary protein, a condition known locally as *nandudu*.

These four children are part of the extended Wandwasi family. This HPI project couple cares for 18 children—their own plus those from two related families who were orphaned when both sets of parents died.

Despite the disparity in their size, the children in the photo above are both nine years old; the boy is healthy, but the girl is malnourished. According to the local project chairperson, Loy Wamboga, the girl's mother has virtually no income and doesn't understand the importance of a balanced diet.

"The girl isn't going to school," Loy says. "She will probably be married at 12 to 14 years of age, and the poverty cycle will continue."

"To expand the school as the children grow— that is my dream."

Blandina Bumbo *(far left)*
HPI Farmer

GOOD MADAM SCHOOL   When times get tough, heroes often emerge. In the YWCA project group outside Mbale, Blandina Bumbo *(above, left)* is a hero who wears a yellow dress and a perpetual smile.

The gift of an HPI dairy cow to Blandina and her husband John set off a wonderful chain of events and unleashed incredible generosity. Thanks to their cow, Anna, the Bumbos suddenly had enough milk for their three children and the two orphans they had adopted *(above)*, with extra left to sell.

Using income from their cow's offspring, Blandina and other HPI project members hired teacher Jane Giddongo *(right)*. She conducts a nursery school for area children, mostly orphans, using a shelter originally constructed for Heifer Project training. The children come to the "Good Madam School" to learn rhymes, songs, the alphabet and how to care for the cow.

It takes Blandina and her helpers about three hours each day to prepare and serve milk porridge to the children *(left)* before the youngsters go home from school. For some, this will be the only hot meal they receive that day.

TRAINING ON THE JOB   Ongoing training in animal breeding, nutrition, health and marketing is vital to the long-term success of HPI projects. Teaching basic record-keeping becomes especially important in countries like Uganda, where half the population is illiterate and handling money is a new experience for many.

Blandina Bumbo's mango tree shades members of the YWCA Project *(left)* during a regular training session on animal nutrition. Trainees learn that a balanced diet—critical to maintain top milk production from dairy cows—involves a lot more than just gathering grass. During this class, experts from the local extension service led a discussion on 17 local varieties of grasses and legumes—how to identify and grow them, their benefits and how they complement one another.

Using their initiative and training in operating a small business, Boniface Ssebabenga and other Heifer Project farmers organized a dairy cooperative. Each morning, the farmers of Kageye village wait their turn to deposit around 80 gallons of milk with the co-op *(right)*. "Since there is no refrigeration, all milk taken in needs to be sold daily," says Bernard Muyeya, director of HPI/Uganda. "Any left over will be boiled. This process can rob roughly 10 percent of the volume through evaporation."

A lactometer measures the purity of milk received, while a basket serves as cash register for milk sold *(below)*. The money it contains reveals the fragile nature of the rural economy—small denomination bills are black and ragged with usage, while the few larger notes remain crisp and clean.

KENYA

East African women are accustomed to bearing heavy burdens, since most of the work for day-to-day survival has always fallen into their hands. Supplying food and water to family and animals, rearing children and taking care of home and garden have long been considered women's tasks. In contrast, men traditionally own all the property. If a husband dies, his land and animals pass to a brother or a son, not to his wife.

Heifer Project's Gender Program is helping to break this mold by encouraging women as well as men to take leadership roles and seek technical training. Sherry Otwoma in western Kenya is a shining example. Sherry serves as chairperson of the Esabalu Self-Help Group, numbering 200 women. More than 100 of these women own dairy cows, a number about to be increased by one as Sherry presides over a pass-on ceremony in her yard (*far right*).

Heifer Project animals have given women in Sherry's group, like widow Juliana Amakundu (*right, above*) and her daughter Judith (*right, below*), their first opportunity to own property. Having an income-producing animal and completing training in its care lead to self-confidence and, in Sherry's case, community leadership. Because these Kenyan women have earned respect, they now have a voice in family financial decisions.

"The approach of HPI's Gender Program is not confrontational," says coordinator Dr. Beth Miller. "Heifer Project points out the benefits for families, how overall food and income production can increase when both men and women are involved. We recognize that women need to be full participants in the struggle against poverty."

EYES OF THE FUTURE   Exuberance, fear, curiosity, uncertainty, playfulness, passion—the eyes of Kenyan school children *(right)* reveal the emotions of children everywhere.

Complex problems, such as rapid population growth, pose an uncertain future for hundreds of millions of youngsters in developing countries. Finding lasting solutions remains a daunting task that demands awareness and sensitivity to cultural traditions.

The large size of families in societies like those in Kenya has traditionally have been dictated by agrarian economics and the low survival rate of children. Children provide cheap labor for daily chores—fetching water and firewood, working fields, cooking meals and tending livestock. More children make possible a larger herd or a bigger farm. With no pensions or social security, parents depend on sons and daughters to care for them in old age. For centuries, along with livestock, the measure of African wealth has been children.

"Education, particularly for women, is absolutely crucial to breaking the cycle of poverty," says Dr. James DeVries, Heifer Project's international programs director. "But world-wide implementation will require time, patience and the support of organizations such as Heifer Project International."

Healthy, happy and hopeful, or hungry and fearful—it's hard to know what fate awaits these Kenyan children. Looking deeply into their eyes is like peering into the future of the world.

HEIFER PROJECT INTERNATIONAL

Heifer Project International's unique and successful approach to ending hunger and poverty has become a model for rural development around the world. Since 1944, HPI has worked with many partner organizations to provide animals and training to four million families in 115 countries. The program promotes self-reliance, which builds self-esteem and helps communities and families lift themselves out of poverty. Milk, eggs, wool, draft power and other benefits from the animals provide families with food and income.

At the heart of HPI's philosophy is the commitment families make to "pass on the gift." As each family shares one or more of its animal's offspring with another family in need, it experiences the dignity and joy of helping others and the original gift is multiplied from generation to generation.

HELPING CHILDREN   Heifer Project began because Dan West, a Church of the Brethren farmer from Indiana, was saddened by the sight of hungry children on both sides of the conflict during the 1936-39 Spanish Civil War. Still today, millions of children in the United States and around the world go to bed hungry every night. Malnourished, they are susceptible to diseases and unable to learn and grow.

HPI project partners tell us that "milk is good medicine." Their children improve with regular, high-quality protein food. With a steady income from the sale of animal products, parents can pay for their children's school fees, clothes and books as well as health care and better housing.

BUILDING COMMUNITY   Communities grow when families come together to discuss their needs, develop a proposal to HPI and work out problems. Local project partners take full responsibility for their projects, setting their own goals and evaluating results. Leadership and technical training begin even before the animals arrive. HPI animals enable individuals to build small businesses that benefit the whole community, while the groups often go on to tackle other challenges.

Using Heifer Project's grassroots approach, people make their own decisions about how to improve their lives. As project partners work together to overcome obstacles, they strengthen their communities and foster local democracy.

PROTECTING THE ENVIRONMENT   By training partners in environmentally sound, sustainable agriculture practices, HPI makes lasting change possible. To preserve fragile land and collect manure efficiently, many HPI partners limit their animals' grazing. They plant fodder trees that nourish the soil and provide cooking fuel and building materials. They take pride in protecting the soil and forests and increasing crop yields through compost and animal manure.

STRENGTHENING FAMILIES   Around the world, women usually tend their family's livestock and crops. Sadly, many have little access to resources and training. Heifer Project ensures that women share in the benefits of training and income. Many projects enable fathers to farm at home rather than seek low-paying seasonal jobs elsewhere. Livestock projects also help curb the urban migration of unemployed rural youth.

YOU CAN MAKE A DIFFERENCE   Heifer Project International depends on individuals, congregations, community groups, schools and companies to carry out its life-changing work. To find out how you can get involved or to learn about fundraising and education programs for your organization, please call or write:

Heifer Project International, Inc.
1015 Louisiana St.
P.O. Box 808
Little Rock, AR 72203-0808

(800) 422-0474
or
(501) 376-6836

Web Site: http://www.heifer.org

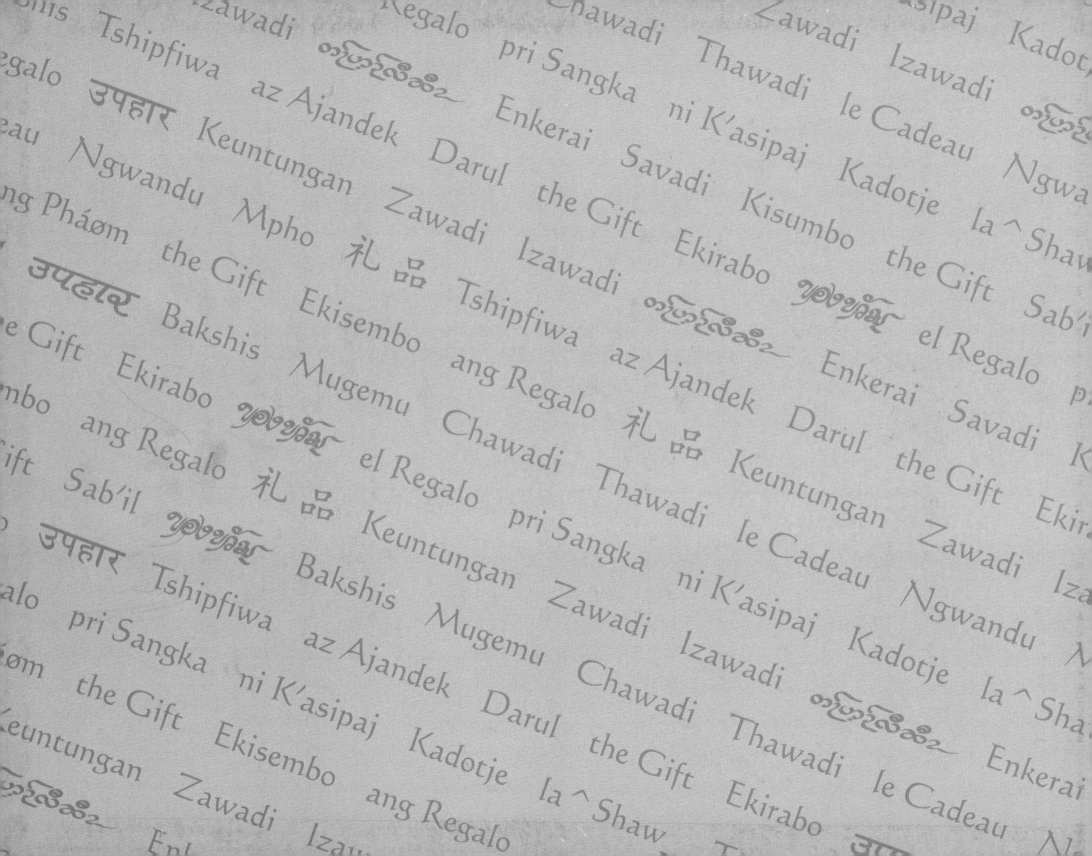